Baboons
and Other Old World Monkeys

Concept and Product Development: Editorial Options, Inc.
Series Designer: Karen Donica
Book Author: Steven A. Horak

For information on other World Book
products, visit us at our Web site at
http://www.worldbook.com

For information on sales to schools and libraries
in the United States, call 1-800-975-3250.

For information on sales to schools and libraries
in Canada, call 1-800-837-5365.

© 2002 World Book, Inc. All rights reserved. This book may not be reproduced, in whole or in part, without the prior written permission from the publisher.

World Book, Inc.
233 N. Michigan Avenue
Chicago, IL 60601

Library of Congress Cataloging-in-Publication Data

Horak, Steven A.
    Baboons and other old world monkeys / [Steven A. Horak].
      p. cm.
    Summary: Presents information about baboons and other Old World monkeys, including their physical characteristics, behavior, and natural environment.
    ISBN 0-7166-1244-0 -- ISBN 0-7166-1223 (set)
    1. Baboons--Juvenile literature. 2. Cercopithecidae--Juvenile literature. [1. Baboons. 2. Monkeys.] I. World Book, Inc. II. Series.

QL737.P93 H67 2002
599.8'6--dc21
                                                                         2001046711

Printed in Malaysia
1 2 3 4 5 6 7 8 9 05 04 03 02

Picture Acknowledgments: Cover: © Ralph A. Reinhold, Animals Animals; © Erwin & Peggy Bauer, Bruce Coleman Inc.; © Angelina Lax, Photo Researchers; © Mark D. Phillips, Photo Researchers; © Norman Owen Tomalin, Bruce Coleman Inc.

© K. & K. Ammann, Bruce Coleman Inc. 15, 23, 53; © Erwin & Peggy Bauer, Bruce Coleman Inc. 13; © Alan D. Carey, Photo Researchers 35; © Nigel J. Dennis, Photo Researchers 61; © Gregory G. Dimijian, Photo Researchers 33, 47; © Gerry Ellis, Minden Pictures 21; © Fletcher & Baylis, Photo Researchers 51; © Michael Freeman, Bruce Coleman Inc. 41; © Barbara Gerlach, Tom Stack & Associates 11; © M. P. Kahl, Bruce Coleman Inc. 19; © G. C. Kelly, Photo Researchers 29; © Frank Krahmer, Bruce Coleman Inc. 27; © Gerard Lacz, Animals Animals 45; © Angelina Lax, Photo Researchers 55; © Werner Layer, Bruce Coleman Collection 57; © Joe McDonald, Animals Animals 25; © Tom McHugh, Photo Researchers 49; © Anthony Mercieca, Photo Researchers 39; © Claus Meyer, Minden Pictures 11; © Mark D. Phillips, Photo Researchers 33; © Ralph A. Reinhold, Animals Animals 17; © Len Rue Jr., Bruce Coleman Inc. 7; © Norman Owen Tomalin, Bruce Coleman Inc. 31, 59; © Wardene Weisser, Bruce Coleman Inc. 37; © Art Wolfe, Photo Researchers 43.

Illustrations: WORLD BOOK illustration by Karen Donica 9. WORLD BOOK illustration by Kersti Mack 62.

World Book's Animals of the World

Baboons
and Other Old World Monkeys

What makes me like you?

World Book, Inc.
A Scott Fetzer Company
Chicago

Contents

What Are Old World Monkeys? 6

Where in the World Do Old World Monkeys Live? 8

How Do Old World and New World Monkeys Differ? 10

Why Do Baboons Make Faces? 12

What Is a Baboon Troop Like? 14

Who Helps with Grooming? 16

Why Do Baboons Bark? 18

How Else Do Baboons Defend Themselves? 20

How Do Baboons Protect Themselves at Night? 22

What Do Baboons Stuff in Their Cheeks? 24

How Do Baboons Raise Their Young? 26

Which Baboon Wears a Cape? 28

Which Old World Monkey Is Bigger Than a Baboon? 30

Why Are Mandrills So Colorful? 32

What Are Macaques? 34

Which "Ape" Isn't Really an Ape? 36

When do I sit as still as a statue?

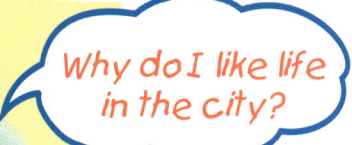

Why do I like life in the city?

Which Old World Monkey Looks Like a Lion? 38

Who Is at Home in the Snow? 40

Where Do Black Mangabeys Hang Out? 42

Who Is the Fastest Old World Monkey? 44

Are Vervet Monkeys Very Vocal? 46

What's So Unusual About De Brazza's Monkeys? 48

What Do Leaf Monkeys Eat? 50

Can Some Monkeys Fly? 52

Which Old World Monkeys Like City Life? 54

Which Langur Wears a Patchwork Coat? 56

How Did the Proboscis Monkey Get Its Name? 58

Are Old World Monkeys in Danger? 60

Old World Monkey Fun Facts 62

Glossary 63

Index / Old World Monkey Classification 64

How can I get your attention?

What Are Old World Monkeys?

Scientists classify all monkeys into one of two main groups. Old World monkeys are one of these groups. The other group is New World monkeys. There are many species, or kinds, of Old World monkeys. Baboons are Old World monkeys. Mandrills and langurs are Old World monkeys, too.

Baboons and most other Old World monkeys are large monkeys. Males are usually much larger than females. Male baboons weigh up to 90 pounds (41 kilograms). All Old World monkeys have 32 teeth.

Baboons and all other monkeys belong to an order of mammals called primates. Primates have large eyes that face forward. They have large brains, too. Most primates can grasp objects with their hands and feet. Many have thumbs that can be placed opposite any of their other fingers. Apes are another kind of primate. You and other humans are primates, too!

Baboon

Where in the World Do Old World Monkeys Live?

Old World monkeys live mostly in parts of Africa and Asia. This is their original range. It was once the only area where they lived. Today, some species live in small areas in other parts of the world, too, such as Europe and the West Indies. But humans brought these monkeys to these places, and most of them are no larger than small preserves.

Most kinds of baboons live only in Africa. The olive baboon, the most common baboon, is found over much of central Africa. One kind of baboon, the hamadryas *(HAM uh DRY uhs)* baboon, is also found in the Arabian Peninsula *(puh NIHN suh luh)*.

Baboons live in a variety of habitats, such as rocky plains, woodlands, and grasslands. In dry areas, they must stay near a constant source of water, such as a lake, a river, or a waterhole. In wet areas, baboons get much of their water from juicy plants and morning dew.

World Map

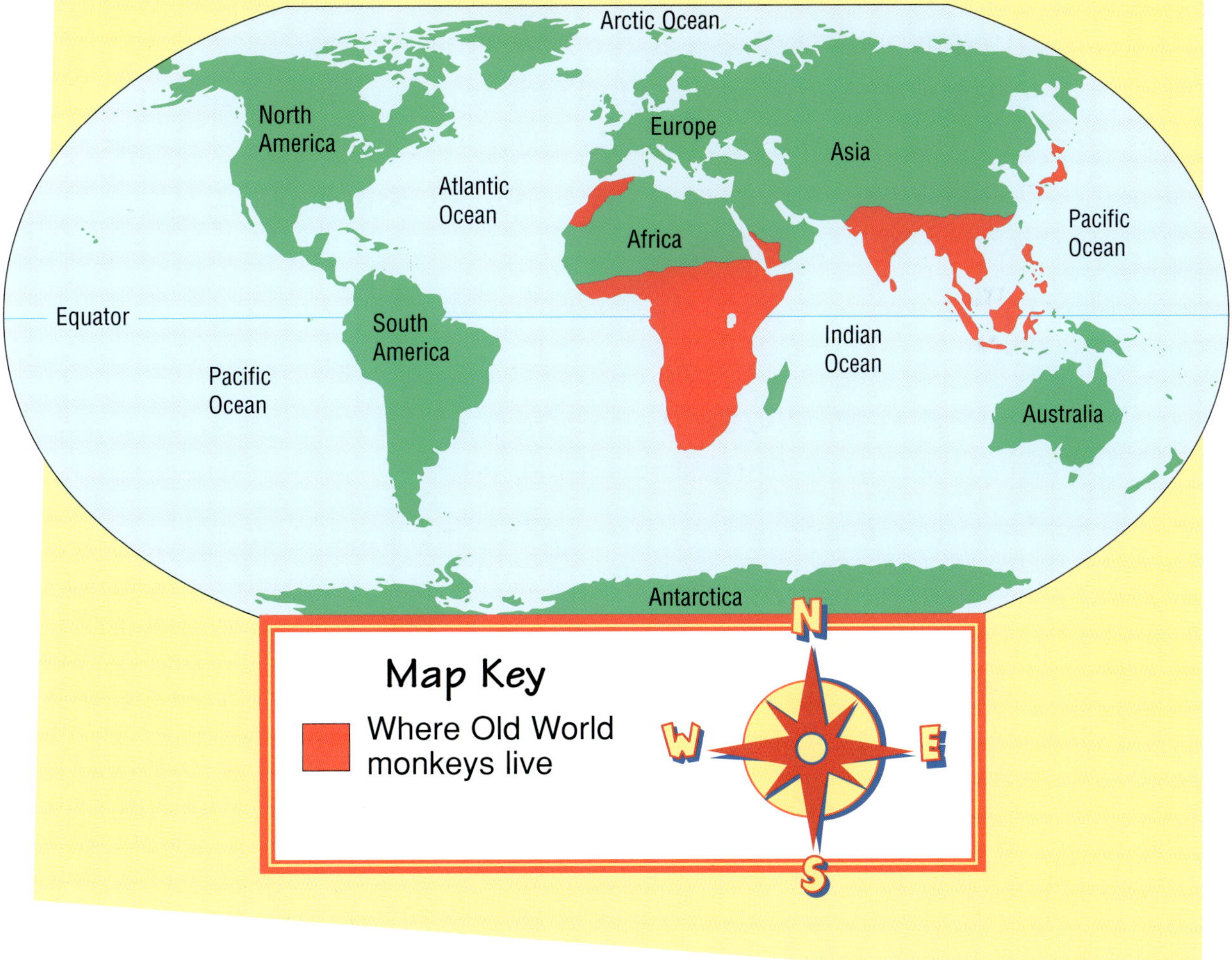

Arctic Ocean
North America
Europe
Asia
Atlantic Ocean
Africa
Pacific Ocean
Equator
South America
Pacific Ocean
Indian Ocean
Australia
Antarctica

Map Key
■ Where Old World monkeys live

N W E S

How Do Old World and New World Monkeys Differ?

Old World monkeys differ from New World monkeys in many ways. One way is where they live. Old World monkeys live in Africa and Asia. New World monkeys live from the southern part of North America to South America.

Look closely at the noses of these two monkeys. Do you see a difference between them? Old World monkeys have narrow noses. New World monkeys have nostrils that are spaced far apart.

Most Old World monkeys are bigger than New World monkeys. All New World monkeys have tails, but not all Old World monkeys do. And no Old World monkey has a prehensile *(pree HEHN suhl)*, or grasping, tail. Some New World monkeys do.

Many Old World monkeys spend most of their time on the ground. But others prefer trees. All New World monkeys spend most of their time in trees.

Old World monkey

New World monkey

Why Do Baboons Make Faces?

Baboons make a lot of faces. Sometimes they look as if they are smiling. Sometimes they raise their eyebrows. Or they can even make a face like the one you see here. Whatever face a baboon makes, the face sends information to other baboons.

Baboons are social animals. They live in troops, or large groups. Good communication between troop members is important. It can help prevent fights. And it can keep everybody safe.

When a baboon makes a face, it is trying to communicate a specific message. If a baboon shows off its sharp teeth, it's telling other baboons, "Be careful or else!" If a baboon grins, it's telling another baboon, "I'm sorry."

What Is a Baboon Troop Like?

A baboon troop can have from 10 to 200 members. Most of these members are adult females and their young. Adult males make up the rest of the troop.

For such a big group, baboon troops are very well organized. Each member has a certain rank, or position. Several dominant adult males lead the troop. These males are the strongest baboons in the troop. It's up to them to keep the troop in order.

The leaders have a lot of responsibilities. They decide where the troop travels, feeds, and sleeps. And they organize the troop's defense against enemies.

It's not all hard work for the leaders though. They get the first pick of food. And there's always a fellow troop member ready to groom, or clean, them. That's not such a bad deal!

Baboon troop

Who Helps with Grooming?

Like all wild animals, baboons can get very dirty. They also can get animals such as insects, ticks, and mites stuck in their fur. These creatures, called parasites *(PAIR uh syts),* bite or suck a baboon's blood. They may even spread diseases. So it's important for a baboon to get rid of these pests.

Luckily, a baboon has help grooming. One baboon helps another groom by carefully picking parasites and dirt out of the other baboon's fur. Grooming is an important part of baboon life. It helps baboons develop strong relationships with one another. It helps keep their relationships strong, too. Usually, lower-ranking members groom higher-ranking members of a baboon troop.

Baboon grooming another

Why Do Baboons Bark?

Every so often, a baboon needs to get a message to the whole troop. But troop members can spread far apart as they search for food. Or, if they are traveling, the baboons may be in a very long line. So what's a baboon to do? That's easy. A baboon barks.

A baboon's bark is a very loud call that sounds like "Wahoo!" Baboons use their booming barks to warn each other when there is danger. Scientists believe that certain barks tell other baboons very specific messages. For example, one kind of bark might alert other baboons that a lion is nearby.

Their loud barks can scare enemies away, too. A baboon also has four canines, which are long, pointed teeth. If an enemy gets too close, a baboon will open its mouth wide and show off its canines. Most enemies know that a baboon's bite is much worse than its bark!

Baboon barking

How Else Do Baboons Defend Themselves?

Baboons have many enemies, including other baboons. Sometimes two males bark at each other when they are competing for the same female. If barking doesn't scare off one of the baboons, the two may fight for dominance.

Baboons will also fight an enemy to defend the troop. But they usually prefer to avoid enemies rather than to fight them. Baboons are fast animals. With their long arms and powerful legs, they can often outrun most enemies.

Baboons are also excellent climbers. They have long tails, which help them keep their balance on branches. If a baboon can't outrun an enemy, it will climb a tree.

Baboons squaring off

How Do Baboons Protect Themselves at Night?

During the day, baboons can climb trees to avoid enemies. But at night they often climb high up to the sides of cliffs or treetops for protection. Once there, baboons settle down and go to sleep.

Climbing so high just to go to sleep might seem like a lot of work. But there's a reason baboons do this. Leopards, lions, and hyenas all hunt baboons. These enemies and others live on the ground. And many of them often hunt at night. So when it gets dark out, baboons go where most of their enemies don't. They go up!

Once on the side of a cliff or in a treetop, baboons are safe from most attacks. Up there, baboons don't have to worry too much about their enemies. And they can get a good night's sleep.

Baboons on a cliff

What Do Baboons Stuff in Their Cheeks?

Baboons and some other Old World monkeys have special pouches that line the insides of their cheeks. Baboons often fill these pouches with their favorite food: fruit.

When baboons feed, it's every baboon for itself. Baboons sometimes even steal each other's food. On top of that, there's always the danger of an enemy prowling nearby. That's why a baboon's cheek pouches can really come in handy. Cheek pouches allow a baboon to gather a lot of food in a short amount of time. The baboon can then store its food there until it's safe to eat.

Besides fruit, baboons also eat leaves, insects, and roots. Baboons also work together to get larger meals. They sometimes hunt in groups for small animals such as young impalas and gazelles.

Baboon eating

How Do Baboons Raise Their Young?

Female baboons, like other Old World monkeys, give birth to one baby at a time. When the baby is born, it is tiny and helpless. It clings to its mother's fur. Like other mammals, the baby baboon depends on its mother's milk for food.

The mother keeps a close eye on her newborn baby. She often carries it under her belly wherever she goes. As the baby grows older, the mother begins to carry it on her back.

A mother baboon can count on fellow troop members to help her care for her baby. Others in the troop sometimes carry the babies, too. When danger is near, the mothers and their young head for cover. Large adult males usually drive away any enemies.

When a young male baboon turns four, it usually leaves the troop and joins another one. Females remain in the same troop for their entire lives.

Baboon with young

Which Baboon Wears a Cape?

Here you see an adult male hamadryas baboon. He has long gray hair that hangs down over his shoulders. Males may not grow this hair until they are 10. In time, it looks just like a cape!

Hamadryas baboons form groups, just as other baboons do. But hamadryas groups are not like other baboon troops. A hamadryas group is called a harem. A harem is made up of several females and their young and one adult male. He is the leader. Sometimes harems come together and form much larger groups.

Hamadryas baboons mainly eat seeds, roots, and leaves. They also eat small mammals and insects. They'll even raid crops and garbage dumps, too.

Hamadryas baboon

Which Old World Monkey Is Bigger Than a Baboon?

A male mandrill is the only monkey that is bigger than a baboon. This powerful Old World monkey lives in dense forests in western Africa. It can grow to a length of 31 inches (79 centimeters) from head to tail. Like baboons, female mandrills are much smaller than males.

A mandrill has a long snout and sharp canines—just as a baboon does. It also has a thick body and arms that are longer than its legs. But instead of a long tail, a mandrill has a short stump.

Like baboons, mandrills spend most of their time on the ground. And like baboons, they also form troops. Mandrill troops can have as many as 95 members.

Mandrills mostly eat fruits and seeds. They also eat insects. Mandrills often find insects to eat by turning over large rocks.

Male mandrill

Why Are Mandrills So Colorful?

Adult male mandrills have long, bluish-white snouts. The snout has a bright red streak right down the middle. It sure catches the eye! And that's exactly what the snout is designed to do.

A male mandrill's color is very important. The more colorful a male is, the more successful he is within a mandrill troop. The males with the most colorful snouts are the most dominant. They lead the troop and protect it from enemies. These males also get the most attention from the females.

Male mandrills also have colorful backsides. They often lead the troop through thick forests. Scientists believe that the bright red and blue make it easier for the rest of the troop to follow.

Male mandrill

What Are Macaques?

Macaques *(muh KAHKS)* are another group of Old World monkeys that are closely related to baboons. Like baboons and mandrills, they have cheek pouches. They are large monkeys, too. Some kinds of macaques can weigh over 30 pounds (14 kilograms).

Macaques are one of the most widespread groups of Old World monkeys. They are found as far west in Africa as Morocco and as far east in Asia as Japan. Most macaques live in Asia.

There are many different kinds of macaques. Most, like this rhesus macaque, live both on the ground and in the trees. Some have long tails, while others have short tails. A few kinds have no tails at all.

Rhesus macaque

Which "Ape" Isn't Really an Ape?

The Barbary *(BAHR buhr ee)* ape is actually a macaque, not an ape. It's often called an ape because, like an ape, it doesn't have a tail. But this macaque, like all monkeys, has very little in common with apes. Apes are bigger and heavier than monkeys. Apes have shorter and wider noses than monkeys. Apes often stand up and walk on two legs. You won't see many monkeys try this!

Barbary apes live in northern Africa. They also live on Gibraltar *(juh BRAWL tuhr),* a rocky peninsula on the southern tip of Spain. These Barbary apes are the only wild monkeys that live in Europe. Humans took them there to live long ago.

Barbary ape

Which Old World Monkey Looks Like a Lion?

For a monkey, the lion-tailed macaque looks a lot like a lion. In fact, that's how it got its name. This macaque has a tuft at the tip of its tail—just like a lion. And like a lion, the lion-tailed macaque has a thick mane around its face.

Lion-tailed macaques live in southern India in trees with flat, broad leaves. They eat, sleep, and travel in small troops. When the troop travels from tree to tree, the males often let out loud calls. They sound like "Whoo!" This lets other lion-tailed macaque troops know to stay away. The males repeat this call over and over. This way everybody gets the message!

Lion-tailed macaque

Who Is at Home in the Snow?

Japanese macaques live farther north than any other monkey or ape. Many live on Honshu Island. It can get very cold on this Japanese island. It can snow a lot there, too. That's why Japanese macaques are often called snow monkeys.

These macaques are well prepared for such harsh weather. They have thick coats that protect them from the cold. When the temperature really drops, Japanese macaques huddle close together. Then they hug one another tightly. Their combined body heat helps keep each other warm.

Many Japanese macaques live near hot springs. Hot springs are pools of water that are heated from below the earth's surface. When Japanese macaques need to heat up in a hurry, they go for a dip. Sometimes they pass hours just relaxing in the steamy water. That's the life!

Japanese macaques

Where Do Black Mangabeys Hang Out?

Black mangabeys *(MANG guh bayz)* hang out high up in the forest canopy in parts of central Africa. The canopy is a thick, rooflike covering formed by several treetops. It provides black mangabeys with almost everything they need. In fact, black mangabeys rarely come to the ground.

Food is never too hard to find for black mangabeys up in the canopy. They pick most of it right off of the trees. These monkeys mainly eat fruits and nuts.

The canopy also provides protection. The bunched-together leaves and branches provide many hiding places. When black mangabeys spot an enemy such as an eagle, they quickly dive for cover.

Black mangabeys live in troops of about 15 members. Adult males often call out a very loud "Whoop-gobble!" This lets other mangabey troops know where they are.

Black mangabey

Who Is the Fastest Old World Monkey?

The large patas monkey of central Africa is the fastest Old World monkey. In fact, it's the fastest of all primates. When a patas monkey gets going, it can run up to 34 miles (55 kilometers) an hour!

Patas monkeys have long heels and short fingers and toes designed for running. And with its long legs, a patas monkey can take some very big strides. The patas monkey uses its great speed to escape from enemies such as jackals and hyenas. This monkey can usually outrun whatever enemy is chasing it.

Sometimes a male patas monkey will even try to get an enemy to chase him. But he's not playing around. He's trying to draw the enemy away from other patas monkeys. The male gets its enemy's attention by bouncing or barking. When the enemy gives chase, the patas monkey runs away.

Patas monkey with baby

Are Vervet Monkeys Very Vocal?

Yes, vervet monkeys are very vocal. Scientists believe they have over 20 different calls. The most important calls are alarm calls. Vervet monkeys have different alarm calls for different enemies. One alarm call might warn, "Up there, a bird of prey!" If a leopard or a hyena is nearby, a different call might say, "Over there, a large enemy!"

Vervet monkeys can be heard throughout many types of African woodlands and swamps. They are found from South Africa to as far north as Ethiopia *(EE thee OH pee uh)*. These common monkeys are also known as grivets, green monkeys, and savannah monkeys.

Vervet monkey

What's So Unusual About De Brazza's Monkeys?

De Brazza's monkeys live in swampy forests in central Africa. They have white beards. And on their foreheads they have patches of orange fur that are shaped like a half moon. But that's not all that's unusual about De Brazza's monkeys.

Unlike most monkeys, De Brazza's monkeys live in family groups. A family group is often made up of an adult male, an adult female, and their young. Sometimes, a family group has more than one adult female—just like a hamadryas baboon harem. A family usually stays in a very small area. They may spend several days snacking on fruit from the same tree.

When a family of De Brazza's monkeys senses danger, its members will sit perfectly still. They can do this for hours. When it is safe to move again, the adult male will jump in circles to let everyone know the danger has passed.

De Brazza's monkey

What Do Leaf Monkeys Eat?

As you might guess, leaf monkeys eat leaves. But eating leaves isn't as easy as it sounds. Leaves are very hard to digest. Luckily, leaf monkeys have stomachs with special compartments that help them digest leaves.

Leaf monkeys eat all kinds of leaves. They enjoy young leaves the most. These tender leaves are much easier on a leaf monkey's stomach.

There are many kinds of leaf monkeys. Some are named langurs *(luhng GOORZ)*, while others are called colobus *(KAHL uh buhs)* monkeys. Many of these monkeys are simply known as leaf monkeys.

The silvered leaf monkey lives in forests high up in the mountains of Southeast Asia. Many live in old-growth forests that have very old and very big trees. There are plenty of leaves to choose from in these trees!

Silvered leaf monkey

Can Some Monkeys Fly?

No! But red colobus monkeys do make some incredible leaps. Sometimes one of these leaps can carry a colobus monkey up to 20 feet (6.1 meters). This Old World monkey lives in the treetops in rain forests and swamps. To get from one tree to the next, a colobus monkey finds a long branch. Next, it springs toward another tree with its arms held out in the air. Finally, it lands on its feet and grabs the new tree with its hands.

A colobus monkey has long legs and a very long tail. This monkey's strong legs help it make such great leaps. A colobus monkey uses its long tail for balance. It keeps this monkey safe as it moves around trees.

Red colobus monkey

Which Old World Monkeys Like City Life?

Hanuman langurs are Old World monkeys that live in India and a few nearby countries. Their habitats include tropical forests, thorny scrub forests, and pine forests. Hanuman langurs can be found from sea level to as high as 14,000 feet (4,267 meters). These langurs live in a wider range of elevations than any other monkey. But even with all those choices, Hanuman langurs often settle down in cities.

It's easy to see why Hanuman langurs like life in the city. In India, these monkeys are considered sacred. People often give them food at temples. At night, the monkeys stretch out and go to sleep on building ledges.

Hanuman langur

Which Langur Wears a Patchwork Coat?

Douc langurs live in tropical rain forests in Southeast Asia. This rare langur looks like no other monkey. In fact, it looks as if it's wearing a costume. It has white whiskers, dark gray shoulders, a light gray stomach, white forearms, red legs, and black hands and feet. That's some combination!

Both males and females share this patchwork coat. Males and females are nearly the same size, too. A douc langur can grow as large as 30 inches (76 centimeters). Its tail is quite long—often as long as its body.

Douc langur

How Did the Proboscis Monkey Get Its Name?

The proboscis *(proh BAHS ihs)* monkey got its name for its unique nose. The word *proboscis* means "long, flexible snout." And that's just what the male proboscis monkey has.

The male proboscis monkey's snout looks a bit like a light bulb. But it acts like a loudspeaker. It helps him make some very loud calls. His booming calls warn others when there is danger.

This large monkey lives in mangrove swamps in Borneo. A male proboscis monkey can weigh up to 52 pounds (24 kilograms). It can be as long as 30 inches (76 centimeters).

Proboscis monkeys are excellent swimmers. They swim in much the same way that dogs do! These monkeys slowly wade into streams and rivers on their two hind legs. When they reach deeper water, they paddle with their hands and feet.

Male proboscis monkey

Are Old World Monkeys in Danger?

Many types of Old World monkeys are in danger of becoming extinct, or no longer existing. Several kinds of colobus monkeys are in danger. Other kinds of Old World monkeys, such as the douc langur, are in danger, too.

Humans are the greatest threat to Old World monkeys. These monkeys are losing their habitats as people clear forests. Some species of Old World monkeys are still legally hunted. Poachers kill others for their fur. Many more are captured and sold illegally as pets.

But there is some good news for Old World monkeys. Many species are now protected by law. Huge preserves have been created that protect the habitats of many Old World monkeys. More efforts like these are needed to ensure that Old World monkeys will be here for a long time to come.

Baby baboon

Old World Monkey Fun Facts

- When a baboon yawns, it is often making a threat.

- Silvered leaf monkeys are born bright orange.

- A male gelada baboon threatens other males by flipping his upper lip up and down.

- De Brazza's monkeys almost never eat just half a fruit.

- Many Old World monkeys bob their heads when they feel threatened.

- Colobus monkeys have no thumbs.

- When in danger, a proboscis monkey troop will often dive into a river.

Glossary

ape A large, tailless primate.

bark To give a short, loud yell.

canines Four long, pointed teeth.

canopy A rooflike covering made by treetops.

cheek pouch A special pouch that lines the inside cheeks of some Old World monkeys.

elevation A height above the earth's surface.

groom To clean and take care of appearance.

habitat The area where an animal lives, such as grasslands or deserts.

harem A group of several female hamadryas baboons, their young, and one adult male.

hot springs A pool of water heated from below the earth's surface.

mammal A warm-blooded animal that feeds its young on the mother's milk.

mangrove A type of tropical tree.

New World monkey A monkey that lives from Mexico to Brazil.

Old World monkey A monkey that lives in parts of Africa and Asia.

original range An area where a species once only lived.

parasites Organisms that live on or in another organism and feed from it.

prehensile Good for grasping or holding onto something.

primate Any of the highest order of mammals, including humans, monkeys, and apes.

proboscis A long, flexible snout.

rank A member's position within a troop.

troop The name for a group of monkeys and certain other kinds of animals.

Index

(**Boldface** indicates a photo, map, or illustration.)

Africa, 8, 10, 30, 34, 36, 42, 44, 46, 48
ape, 6, 36, 40
arms, 22, 30, 52, 56
Asia, 8, 10, 34, 50, 56

baboon, 6, **7**, 8, 12, **13**, 14, **15**, 16, **17**, 18, **19**, 20, **21**, 22, **23**, 24, **25**, 26, **27**, 28, **29**, 30, 34, **61**
baby, 26, **27**, 28, 30, 32, 38, 42, 48
Barbary ape, 36, **37**
black mangabey, 42, **43**
Borneo, 58

color, 32, 48, 56
colobus monkey, 50, 52, **53**, 60
communication, 12, 18, **19**, 22, 38, 42, 44, 46, 58

De Brazza's monkey, 48, **49**
douc langur, 56, **57**, 60

enemy, 14, 18, 20, 22, 24, 26, 32, 42, 44, 46, 48, 58
Ethiopia, 46
Europe, 8, 36

feeding habits, 8, 24, **25**, 26, 28, 30, 42, 48, 50, 54
feet, 6, 44, 52, 56, 58
fur, 16, 26, 28, 40, 48, 56, 60

Gibraltar, 36
grooming, 14, 16, **17**
group, 12, 14, **15**, 16, 18, 20, 22, 24, 26, 28, 32, 38, 42, 48

habitat, 8, 10, 30, 38, 40, 42, 46, 48, 50, 52, 54, 56, 58, 60
hamadryas, 8, 28, **29**
hands, 6, 44, 52, 56, 58
Hanuman langur, 54, **55**
Honshu Island, 40
human, 6, 8, 36, 60

India, 38, 54

Japan, 34, 40
Japanese macaque, 40, **41**

langur, 6, 50, 54, 56
leaf monkey, 50, **51**
legs, 22, 30, 36, 44, 52, 56, 58
lion-tailed macaque, 38, **39**
living habits, 14, 20, **21**, 22, **23**, 24, 34, 40

macaque, 34, **35**, 36, **37**, 38, **39**, 40, **41**
mandrill, 6, 30, **31**, 32, **33**, 34
Morocco, 34
movement, 20, 22, 36, 38, 44, 52, 58

New World monkey, 6, 10, **11**

North America, 10
nose, 10, 30, 32, 36, 58

Old World monkey, 6, 8, 10, **11**, 24, 26, 30, 34, 38, 44, 52, 54, 60
olive baboon, 8

parasites, 16
patas monkey, 44, **45**
pouch, 24, 34
primate, 6, 44
proboscis monkey, 58, **59**
protection, 22, 42, 60

size, 6, 10, 30, 34, 36, 56, 58
snout, 30, 32, 58
sounds, 12, 18, **19**, 22, 38, 44, 46, 58
South Africa, 46
South America, 10
Spain, 36
species, 6, 8, 60

tail, 10, 20, 22, 30, 34, 36, 38, 52, 56
teeth, 6, 12, 18, 22, 30
troop, 12, 14, **15**, 16, 18, 20, 22, 24, 26, 28, 32, 38, 42

vervet monkey, 46, **47**

world map, **9**

For more information about Old World monkeys, try these resources:

Apes and Other Hairy Primates, by Richard Platt, Dorling Kindersly, 2001

Gorilla, Monkey & Ape, an Eyewitness Book, Dorling Kindersly, 2000

A Visual Introduction to Monkeys and Apes, Checkmate Books, 2000

http://school.discovery.com/homeworkhelp/worldbook/atozscience/m/367940.html

http://www.mc.maricopa.edu/academic/cult_sci/anthro/primates/old_monkeys.html

http://www.zoobooks.com/twentyarchive/Old%20world%20Monkeys/print/questions.html

Old World Monkey Classification

Scientists classify animals by placing them into groups. The animal kingdom is a group that contains all the world's animals. Phylum, class, order, and family are smaller groups. Each phylum contains many classes. A class contains orders, an order contains families, and a family contains individual species. Each species also has its own scientific name. Here is how the animals in this book fit in to this system.

Animals with backbones and their relatives (Phylum Chordata)

Mammals (Class Mammalia)

Primates (Order Primates)

Old World Monkeys (Family Cercopithecidae)

Barbary ape	*Macaca sylvanus*
Black mangabey	*Cercocebus aterrimus*
De Brazza's monkey	*Cercopithecus neglectus*
Douc langur	*Pygathrix nemaeus*
Gelada	*Theropithecus gelada*
Hamadryas baboon	*Papio hamadryas*
Hanuman langur	*Semnopithecus entellus*
Japanese macaque	*Macaca fuscata*
Lion-tailed macaque	*Macaca silenus*
Mandrill	*Mandrillus sphinx*
Olive baboon	*Papio anubis*
Patas monkey	*Erythrocebus patas*
Proboscis monkey	*Nasalis larvatus*
Rhesus macaque	*Macaca mulatta*
Silvered leaf monkey	*Trachypithecus cristatus*
Vervet monkey	*Cercopithecus aethiops*
Red colobus monkey	*Procolobus badius*